CAR CULTURE

Edited by Marla Hamburg Kennedy

Howard Greenberg Gallery Photography Series

GIBBS·SMITH

➔P

PUBLISHER

Salt Lake City

Published by
Gibbs Smith, Publisher
P.O. Box 667
Layton, Utah 84041
See our Web site: www.gibbs-smith.com

Book design by David Charlsen, San Francisco, California

Printed and bound in Hong Kong

Library of Congress Cataloging-in-Publication Data

Car culture / edited by Marla Hamburg Kennedy. — 1st ed.
   p. cm.
  ISBN 0-87905-846-3
  1. Photography, Artistic. 2. Photography of automobiles. 3. Automobiles—Social
aspects—United States—Pictorial works. I. Kennedy, Marla Hamburg.
  TR650.C333 1998
  779'.9629222—dc21   98-14014
                            CIP

First Edition
02 01 00 99 98 5 4 3 2 1

CAR CULTURE
THE AUTOMOBILE IN TWENTIETH-CENTURY PHOTOGRAPHY

The car and the camera—two machines that have revolutionized modern life—have a special and often intimate relationship. Although the camera's invention preceded the car's by about a half century, not long after the auto's appearance, photography became one of the primary chroniclers of "car culture."

Among the pioneering images of the automobile, Robert Demachy's 1904 *Speed* (p. 43) reflects conflicting attitudes towards the motorcar. On the one hand, Demachy looked to the past: his atmospheric gum-bichromate process is meant to impart esthetic legitimacy to the photograph by making it appear like a print or engraving. On the other, Demachy was an avid motorist, and this race car, mysteriously emerging from darkness, seems to herald the dawning of a century of energy and dynamism. In much the same terms, Karl Benz, who many regard as the true father of the automobile, dramatically described his invention on New Year's Eve in 1879: "We were . . . standing in front of the engine as if it were a great mystery. . . . My heart was pounding. I turned the crank. The engine started to go 'put-put-put' and music of the future sounded with regular rhythm. . . . Suddenly the bells began to ring—New Year's Eve bells. We felt they were not only ringing in a new year, but a new era."

Optimism, even euphoria, often characterized the early stages of this "new era." The artists of Italian Futurism, the art movement most enamored with modern technology, proclaimed: "The world's magnificence has been enriched by a new beauty: the beauty of speed . . . a roaring motorcar . . . is more beautiful than the Victory of Samothrace." Jacques-Henri Lartigue's *Grand Prix of the Automobile Club of France* (p. 44), done in 1912 during the heyday of Futurism, captures speed's allure and immediacy in a blurred and cropped "snapshot." Thirty-five years later, Ted Croner perpetuated the seduction of speed, converting a New York City taxi into a blazing projectile (p. 49).

Throughout photographic history, the car was often treated as a formal object, a provocative visual resource. Even in images of immobile autos, sometimes severely cropped, such as Paul Strand's 1920 *Wire Wheel* (p. 23), the car could embody the ordered rationality and classical beauty of mechanical objects. Intriguingly, Strand also celebrated this "machine esthetic" in abstracted photos of the camera itself.

Of course, attitudes towards the car were not always so positive, especially after a world war and an economic depression sobered man's faith in technological progress. Photographs from the 1930s, especially those done in the United States for the Farm Security Administration, poignantly record the life of poverty-stricken, nomadic workers, as in Arthur Rothstein's *Vernon Evans, Migrant to Oregon Tenant Farmer on Moving His Household, Hamilton* (p. 66). These are the migrant laborers of John Steinbeck's 1939 novel *Grapes of Wrath*, for which "the highway became their home and movement their medium of expression." The American Communist party, stirred by John Ford's 1940 film version of this alleged indictment of American capitalism, arranged to have it screened in the Soviet Union. When the Russian viewers voiced astonishment at how even the poorest Americans had cars, the film was pulled from distribution.

Margaret Bourke-White's 1937 *At the Time of the Louisville Flood* (p. 32), done for *Life* magazine, turns a compassionate scene—Ohio River flood victims awaiting government relief—into an ironic depression commentary. The image pits advertising fantasy against cold reality; "haves" against "have-nots"; those with cars against those without. A looming billboard (something to be seen from a car) portrays an all-too-happy, smiling, white American family, with requisite girl, boy, and dog, off on a carefree jaunt in the motorcar. Below is a grim row of apparently dispossessed blacks, whose thoughts are probably not on leisurely automotive adventure but on basic food and shelter.

Is Bruce Davidson's early 1960s *Couple in and around a Station Wagon* (p. 1) the "American" dream come true spelled out in Bourke-White's billboard? Certainly the signs are there: car, or better yet, station wagon that takes the family, mostly smiling, on an outing. But matters seem to have gotten out of hand, as seven kids, some shoeless, not all cheerful, drape the car. Compare this with a publicity shot from the Standard Oil Company (p. 6). Headed by a "snapshooting" dad, an American family, maintaining the two-child rule, makes a gas-fueled pilgrimage to the government responsible for "the highest standard of living."

It is no accident that so many auto images come from the fifties and sixties, when a booming economy of returning vets, fine-tuned production, and clever marketing and advertising made the car a central fact of American culture. Because it offered instant mobility and possible adventure, the automobile symbolized a "freedom"—political, social, cultural, and economic—that had been cramped and threatened by war and economic deprivation.

Cars were everywhere and the world changed to accommodate them. For Ed Clark, the auto might provide the freedom to enjoy leisure and recreation, but since so many people had vehicles, the liberating road became a clogged highway (p. 8). Dan Weiner's 1954 photograph of a worshipful crowd gathered around a car on display at GM's "Motorama" (p. 22) illustrates the modern idea that technology had become the new secular religion. Ernst Haas's 1951 photo *Drive-in Church* (p. 46) eerily confirms and refutes this principle. In addition to being a church, the automobile could be a dining room and bed-room, as Davidson indicates in photos of a drive-in restaurant and the back seat as trysting spot (pp. 36, 37).

Elliott Erwitt also explored the kiss in the car motif (p. 10). The Davidson is marked by passion, and some shamelessness and desperation, as low-class lovers, one shirtless and tattooed, embrace in a car moving down the highway. Erwitt's is far more romantic. A kiss reflected in the car's side-view mirror recalls glamorous stars on a movie screen, and the circular mirror visually rhymes with a sun setting in the water beyond. Love for and love in the car are ubiquitous themes. If "auto-eroticism" is the stuff of photos, as well as of other art, movies, literature, and pop music, from F. Scott Fitzgerald through the Beach Boys to *Crash*, it's because it's the stuff of life.

Sid Avery's shot of Rock Hudson washing his car (p. 16) offers a hilarious array of fifties-culture symbols, fusing American dreams purveyed by Hollywood, Detroit, and Madison Avenue. Here's a famous celebrity—a shirtless, short-pants Rock Hudson, barrel-chested and stomach sucked in—whose attachment to the car is so strong that, like most American men, he takes pleasure in washing the car himself. The strategic placement of the hose, suggestive of a male body part (like Oldsmobile's rocket hood ornament), confirms that this is the American love affair with the car personified. We're in California, a land of glamor, fantasy, and opportunity, where conspicuous consumption and display reign. A good choice for this sunny clime, the convertible amplifies feelings of intoxication, romance, power, and freedom, and affords an exhilarating dose of ostentatious exhibitionism. Ultimately, the photo is more fiction than fact, epitomized by the eventual uncovering of hunk Rock's true sexual inclinations.

Ray Fisher's *JFK in a Convertible* (p. 64) brims with early sixties Camelot hopefulness and happiness: adoring crowds cheer the youthful President Kennedy in an open motorcade. When this photo was taken, who could have imagined that the extroversion, youth, and vitality incarnated by JFK in the convertible would tragically end? A decade of promise became a decade of turbulence. The escalating Vietnam War, assassinations, and protests and strikes were followed by oil shortages, pollution alerts, automotive and highway safety questions, and sweeping recalls. Even convertibles temporarily faded from the scene. The modern world's fluctuating faith in technology was shaken yet again. Contemporary car photography would express this uncertainty in images often fraught with ambivalence and instability.

No one sensibility dominates the history of car photography. But throughout, photographers have paid close attention to the extended meanings of auto culture. While the automobile's apparent function is transportation, it carries a symbolic weight far beyond its utilitarianism, providing "transport" that is as much psychological and emotional as it is geographical. As a key ingredient in the rites and rituals of modern society, the car helps mark our social, sexual, political, and economic passages and milestones. In many of these rituals, the camera often comes along to record, provide proof, and ultimately aid in their memory. With attitudes as wide-ranging as adulation, appreciation, wit, irony, cynicism, and hostility, photographs document man's provocative relationship with the car and its culture.

—Gerald Silk
author of *Automobile and Culture*

Bruce Davidson 1

2 Anonymous (Underwood Studios)

Martin Munkacsi 3

6   Anonymous (Standard Oil of New Jersey Collection)

Ralph Eugene Meatyard

12   Zoltan Glass

Elliott Erwitt

Inge Morath **15**

Sid Avery

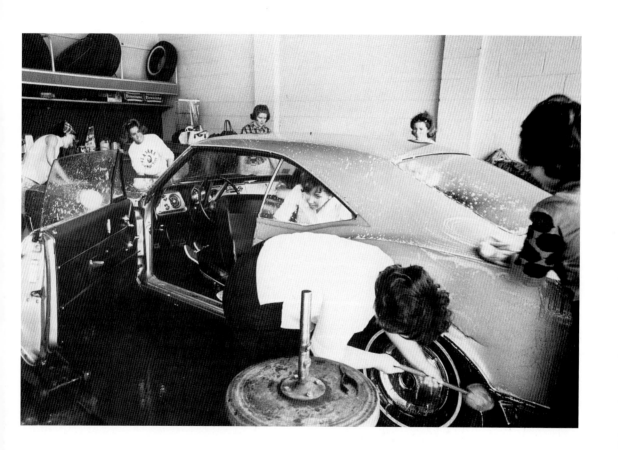

Hiroshi Hamaya

(*Following pages:* George Tice) **17**

William Klein

Dan Weiner

Wright Morris

Inge Morath **31**

WORLD'S

Margaret Bourke-White

Danny Lyon

SHE GOT ME THIS MORNING,
BUT I'LL GET HER TO-NIGHT.

JUST MARRIED

'19 SCENIC '58
CC250
NEW HAMPSHIRE

John Collins

Robert Demachy **43**

44 Jacques-Henri Lartigue

Garry Winogrand

Ted Croner **49**

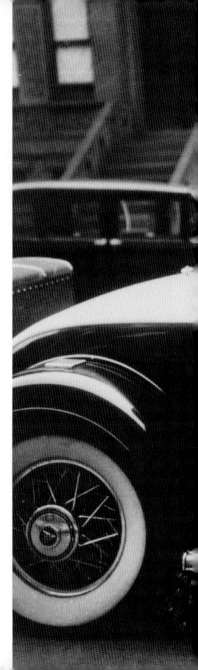

Walker Evans

Henri Cartier-Bresson

Louis Faurer

Arthur Rothstein

68 Sol Libsohn

PHOTOGRAPHERS AND CREDITS

Copyrights rest with the artist, estate of artist, or copyright holder.

Anonymous (6)
> Courtesy Standard Oil of New Jersey Collection
> Photographic Archives, University of Louisville

Anonymous (2)
> Underwood Studios
> Courtesy Keith De Lellis Gallery, New York

Sid Avery (16)
> Courtesy Motion Picture and Television Photo Archive, Van Nuys, California

Lillian Bassman (13)
> Courtesy Howard Greenberg Gallery, New York

Margaret Bourke-White (32)
> Courtesy Life Magazine © Time Inc

Henri Cartier-Bresson (60)
> Courtesy Magnum Photos

Ed Clark (8)
> Courtesy Life Magazine © Time Inc.

John Collins (40)
> Courtesy Howard Greenberg Gallery, New York

Gordon Coster (63)
> Courtesy Keith De Lellis Gallery, New York

Ted Croner (49)
> Courtesy Howard Greenberg Gallery, New York

Bruce Davidson (1, 36, 37)
> Courtesy Magnum Photos

Robert Demachy (43)
> Courtesy Howard Greenberg Gallery, New York

Elliott Erwitt (10, 14, 30, 39)
> Courtesy Magnum Photos

Walker Evans (25, 54)
    Courtesy Howard Greenberg Gallery, New York

Louis Faurer (front cover, 62)
    Courtesy Howard Greenberg Gallery, New York

Ray Fisher (64)
    © Ray Fisher
    Courtesy artist and Howard Greenberg Gallery, New York

Zoltan Glass (12)
    Courtesy Michael Hoppen Photography, London

John Gutmann (55)
    Courtesy artist and Fraenkel Gallery, San Francisco

Ernst Haas (5, 46)
    Courtesy Haas Studio, New York

Hiroshi Hamaya (17)
    Courtesy Magnum Photos

Andre Kertesz (24, back cover)
    Courtesy Robert Gurbo and Estate of Andre Kertesz, New York

William Klein (20, 41)
    Courtesy Howard Greenberg Gallery, New York

Dorothea Lange (29)
    © The Dorothea Lange Collection
    The Oakland Museum of California, City of Oakland
    Gift of Paul S. Taylor

Jacques-Henri Lartigue (44)
    Photographie J.H. Lartigue
    © Ministère de la Culture—France / A.A.J.H.L.

Arthur Leipzig (27)
    Courtesy Howard Greenberg Gallery, New York

Leon Levinstein (35)
    Courtesy Howard Greenberg Gallery, New York

Sol Libsohn (57, 68)
    Courtesy artist and Howard Greenberg Gallery, New York

Danny Lyon (34)
    Courtesy Magnum Photos

Mary Ellen Mark (21)
Courtesy Howard Greenberg Gallery, New York

Ralph Eugene Meatyard (7)
Courtesy Estate of Ralph Eugene Meatyard and Howard Greenberg Gallery, New York

Barbara Morgan (56)
Copyright © 1939, 1980 Barbara Morgan Archives
Courtesy Howard Greenberg Gallery, New York

Inge Morath (15, 31)
Courtesy Magnum Photos and Howard Greenberg Gallery, New York

Wright Morris (28)
Courtesy Howard Greenberg Gallery, New York

Martin Munkacsi (3)
Courtesy Estate of Martin Munkacsi and Howard Greenberg Gallery, New York

Frank Paulin (53)
Courtesy artist and Howard Greenberg Gallery, New York

Thomas Roma (9)
Courtesy artist and Howard Greenberg Gallery, New York

Arthur Rothstein (66)
Courtesy Grace Rothstein and Howard Greenberg Gallery, New York

Paul Strand (23)
Wire Wheel, New York, c. 1920
© 1976, Aperture Foundation Inc., Paul Strand Archive

George Tice (18)
Courtesy artist and Howard Greenberg Gallery, New York

James VanDerZee (50)
Courtesy Donna Messenden VanDerZee and Howard Greenberg Gallery, New York

Dan Weiner (22, 47)
Courtesy Sandra Weiner and Howard Greenberg Gallery, New York

Garry Winogrand (48)
© The Estate of Garry Winogrand
Courtesy Fraenkel Gallery, San Francisco

Marion Post Wolcott (59)
Courtesy Linda Wolcott-Moore Fine Art Photography